CRAYFISH

Life Cycles

Jason Cooper

Rourke Publishing LLC
Vero Beach, Florida 32964

www.rourkepublishing.com

PHOTO CREDITS: Cover © James H. Carmichael; pp. 14, 18 © Barry Mansell; pp. 4, 6, 7, 8, 22 (stage 4) © Lynn M. Stone; pp. 10, 12, 16, 22 (stages 1 & 2) © Breck P. Kent; p. 20 © James H. Carmichael; pp. 13, 22 (stage 3) © Alan Blank/Bruce Coleman, Inc.; p. 19 © Gary Meszaros/Bruce Coleman, Inc.

Editor: Frank Sloan

Cover and page design by Nicola Stratford

Library of Congress Cataloging-in-Publication Data

Cooper, Jason, 1942-
Crayfish / Jason Cooper.
p. cm. -- (Life cycles)
Includes bibliographical references (p.).
Summary: A basic introduction to crayfish, focusing on their physical characteristics, habitat, diet, activities, life cycle, and reproduction.
ISBN 1-58952-704-6 (hardcover)
1. Crayfish--Life cycles--Juvenile literature. [1. Crayfish.] I. Title. II. Series: Cooper, Jason, 1942- Life cycles.
QL444.M33C669 2003
595.3'84--dc21

2003011548

Printed in the USA

CG/CG

Table of Contents

Crayfish look like little lobsters with their pincers and hard, jointed shells.

Crayfish

Crayfish are not fish at all. They are little cousins of lobsters. In fact, crayfish look very much like lobsters. Lobsters are bigger, and they live in salt water. Most of the more than 500 **species** of crayfish live in fresh water.

Both crayfish and lobsters belong to the animal group called **crustaceans**. Crustaceans don’t have a skeleton of bones. Instead, they have a hard outer shell. The shell supports their body. It also gives crustaceans a lightweight covering of armor.

Like other crustaceans, a crayfish has a head with eyes on stalks and two pair of jointed antennas. The antennas help a crayfish sense the things around it, such as water movement and temperature.

Lobster or crayfish? This is the sea-loving Atlantic lobster.

Crayfish have antennas to help them know what is around them.

In addition to having antennas, crayfish bodies have tiny bristles. The bristles also help the crayfish sense things.

The pincers of a crayfish open and snap shut like pliers.

Crayfish, also known as crawfish or crawdads, have several **appendages**. Appendages are long objects that reach out from the main body of the animal. Eight of the crawfish's appendages, for example, are walking legs. But a crayfish also has appendages that help it grasp food and pass it forward.

Two other appendages are the claws, or **pincers**. Pincers help crayfish catch food and fight **predators**.

A crayfish carries her eggs under her tail.

From Egg to Adult

A mother crayfish generally lays from 80 to 200 eggs, but the number depends upon the species. The mother carries the eggs under her tail. The eggs may hatch in two weeks, or they may hatch in 20. It depends upon water temperature and the species of crayfish.

Baby crawfish look like their parents, except that they are very small. For 10 days or as many as 60 days, baby crawfish stay on their mother. They cling to appendages called **swimmerets**.

Even though a crawfish body grows, its shell doesn't. As the crayfish body becomes tighter and tighter within the shell, the shell cracks open! The crawfish crawls out of the old shell.

Newborn crayfish hold on to their mother.

A crayfish sheds its old shell when its body grows too large for it.

The crayfish hides while a new, larger shell grows. This change in shells is called **molting**. During its lifetime, a crawfish molts several times.

This crayfish isn't sunburned or cooked. Some kinds of crayfish are just more brightly colored than others.

Most crawfish are adults at the age of about six months. Then they are old enough to take a mate of their own. Most species of crawfish live for less than two years.

As adults, most kinds of crawfish are between 2 and 6 inches (5 and 15 centimeters) long. But the animal world is full of exceptions. The Tasmanian giant freshwater crayfish, sometimes called a lobster, has reached 32 inches (80 cm) and 12 pounds (5 kilograms)!

A hungry crayfish grabs a worm in its pincer. Crayfish eat plant material, too.

The Lives of Crayfish

Crayfish eat both plant and animal matter. Crayfish like such creatures as snails, minnows, and worms.

Crayfish are generally **aquatic** animals. They live in swamps, marshes, ponds, streams, and rivers. Blind crawfish live in underground streams in caves. They have lost the need for eyesight in their dark surroundings.

A few crayfish species mix their time between water and dry land. The common chimney crayfish dig chimney-like burrows deep enough to hit water. But at night these crayfish crawl upward from their wet basements onto dry land.

The blind cave crayfish has eyes, but they do not work. Cave crayfish live in a world of darkness.

A crayfish crawls out of its chimney onto dry land.

Crayfish live throughout most of the world. About 350 kinds live in the United States, with the greatest number in the Southeast.

Crayfish like to hide, but when found, they defend themselves with their pincers.

Crayfish lead fairly secret lives in the wild. They are small, and they hide easily under rocks, in burrows, and in mud. Scientists in the United States continue to discover “new” crayfish species almost every year!

A few scientists aren’t the only ones looking for wild crayfish. They’re favorite **prey** of raccoons, turtles, alligators, herons, and people. In fact, crayfish are so popular in parts of the Southeast that they are raised on crayfish farms!

Stage 1:
Crayfish begin life in eggs

Stage 2:
Newborn crayfish cling to their mother

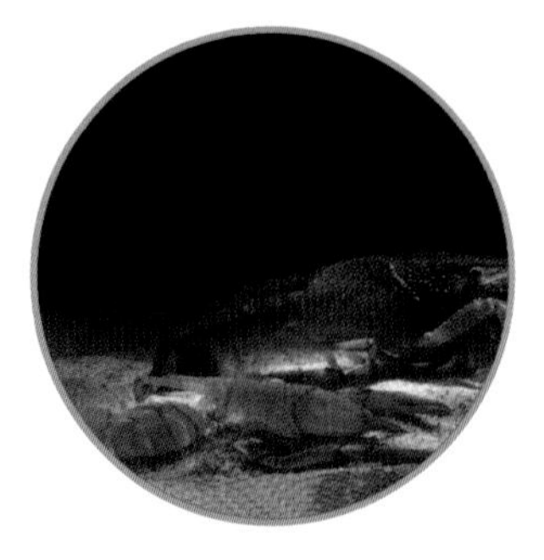

Stage 3:
Crayfish grow and shed their shells

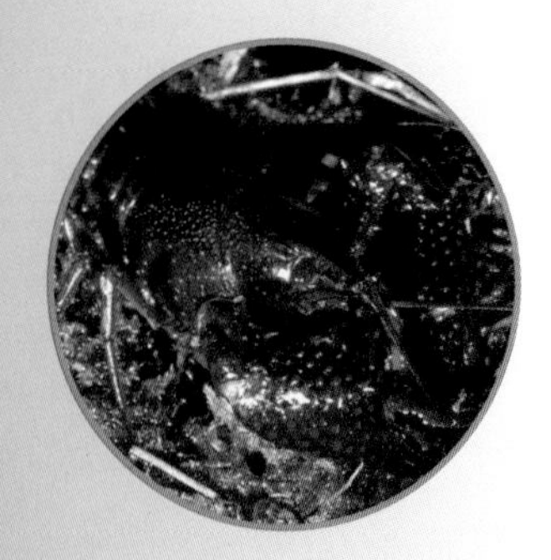

Stage 4:
Adult crayfish can start a new cycle of life

Glossary

appendages (uh PEN dij ez) — finger-like or leg-like body parts attached to the main body of certain animals

aquatic (uh KWAT ick) — refers to animals that live most or all their lives in water

crustaceans (kres TAY shunz) — a group of cold-blooded, boneless animals that have jointed shells and appendages

molting (MOLT ing) — to be in the act of changing from an old shell or skin into a new one

pincers (PIN churz) — claw-like appendages of crayfish that open and close like pliers

predators (PRED uh turz) — animals that kill other animals for food

prey (PRAY) — an animal that is hunted for food by another animal

species (SPEE sheez) — within a closely related group of plants or animals, one certain kind, such as a blind cave crayfish

swimmerets (SWIM uh retz) — appendages of certain crustaceans that aid in swimming and the transport of young

Index

Further Reading

Blaxland, Beth. *Crustaceans, Crabs, Crayfishes and Their Relatives.* Chelsea House, 2002
Grimm, Phyllis W. *Crayfish.* Lerner, 2000
Morgan, Sally. *Crabs and Crustaceans.* Thameside Press, 2001

Websites to Visit

www.mackers.com/crayfish/
http://crayfish.byu.edu/crayhome.htm

About the Author

Jason Cooper has written several children's books about a variety of topics for Rourke Publishing, including the recent series *Life Cycles* and *Fighting Forces.* Cooper travels widely to gather information for his books.